FIGHTING THE BIG C

WHAT CANCER DOES TO THE BODY

BIOLOGY 6TH GRADE

Children's Biology Books

Speedy Publishing LLC
40 E. Main St. #1156
Newark, DE 19711
www.speedypublishing.com

n this book, we're going to talk about what cancer does to the body. So, let's get right to it!

Cancer is a type of disease that begins with abnormal cells that are caused by mutations. Most of the time our healthy cells can protect us from these unhealthy cells. However, sometimes the unhealthy cells begin to grow in an uncontrolled way. Eventually, these growths form tumors and then the cancer sometimes spreads to other parts of the body.

Cancer cells - 3d rendered illustration.

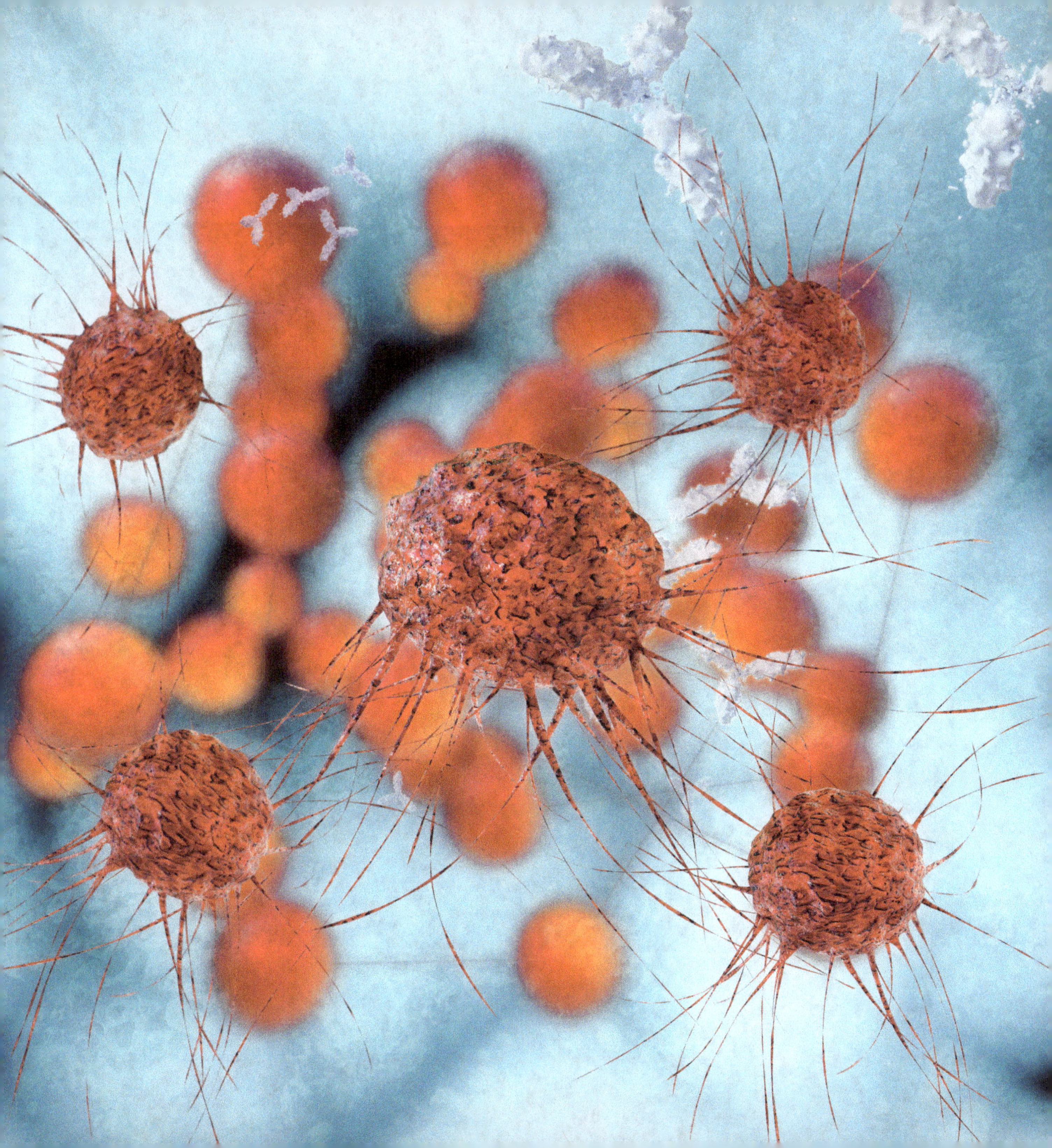

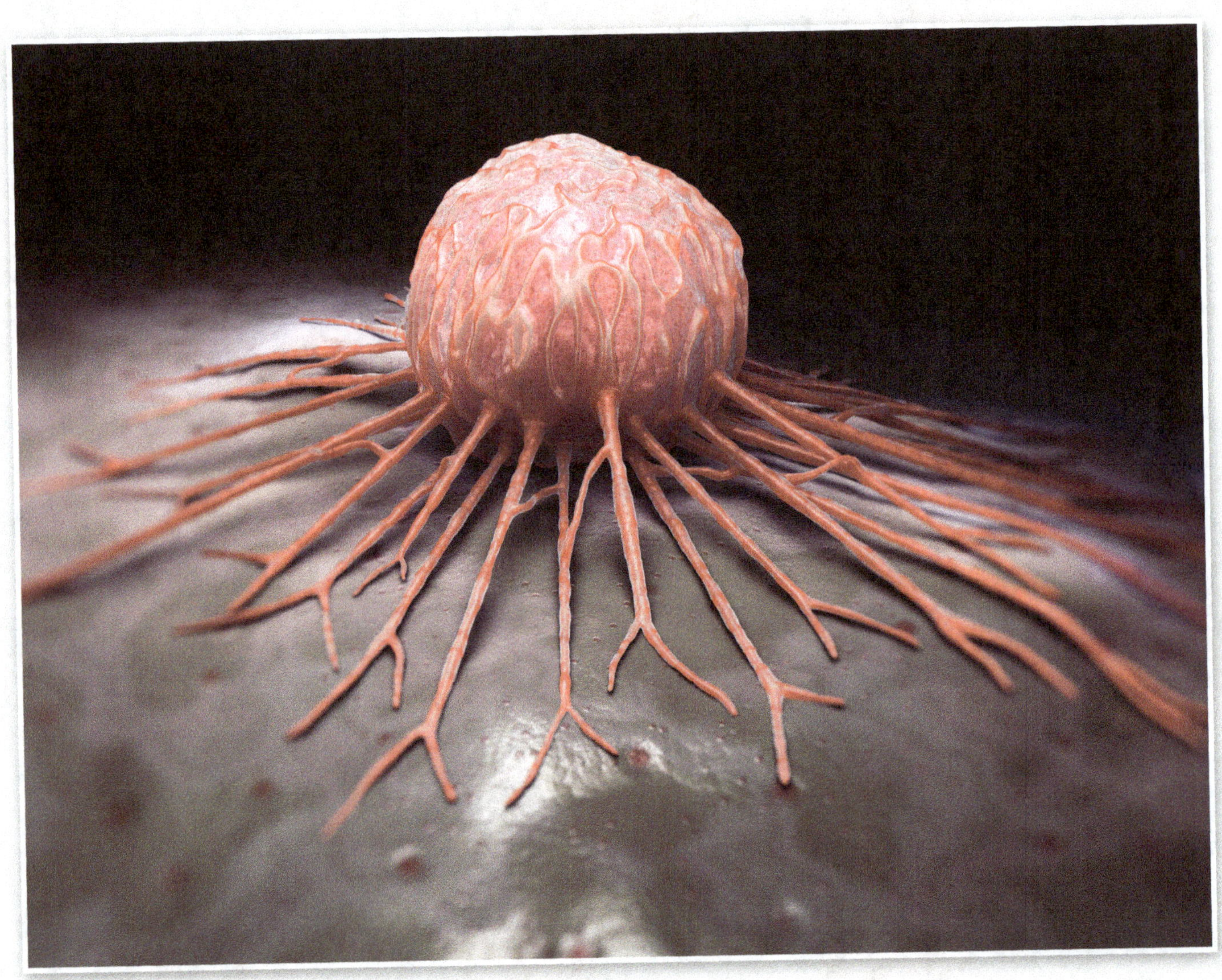

By the time this happens, the person who has cancer is very sick and might not even know it. The cancer cells destroy healthy cells and tissues as they spread.

Cancer cell.

There are over 200 different forms of cancer. Some tissues in the body are more vulnerable to cancers than others. Some cancers are very slow growing and can be treated and stopped if found early enough. Other types of cancers are very aggressive and difficult to treat. About 40% of the people on Earth will have some type of cancer or more than one type at some point during their lifetimes.

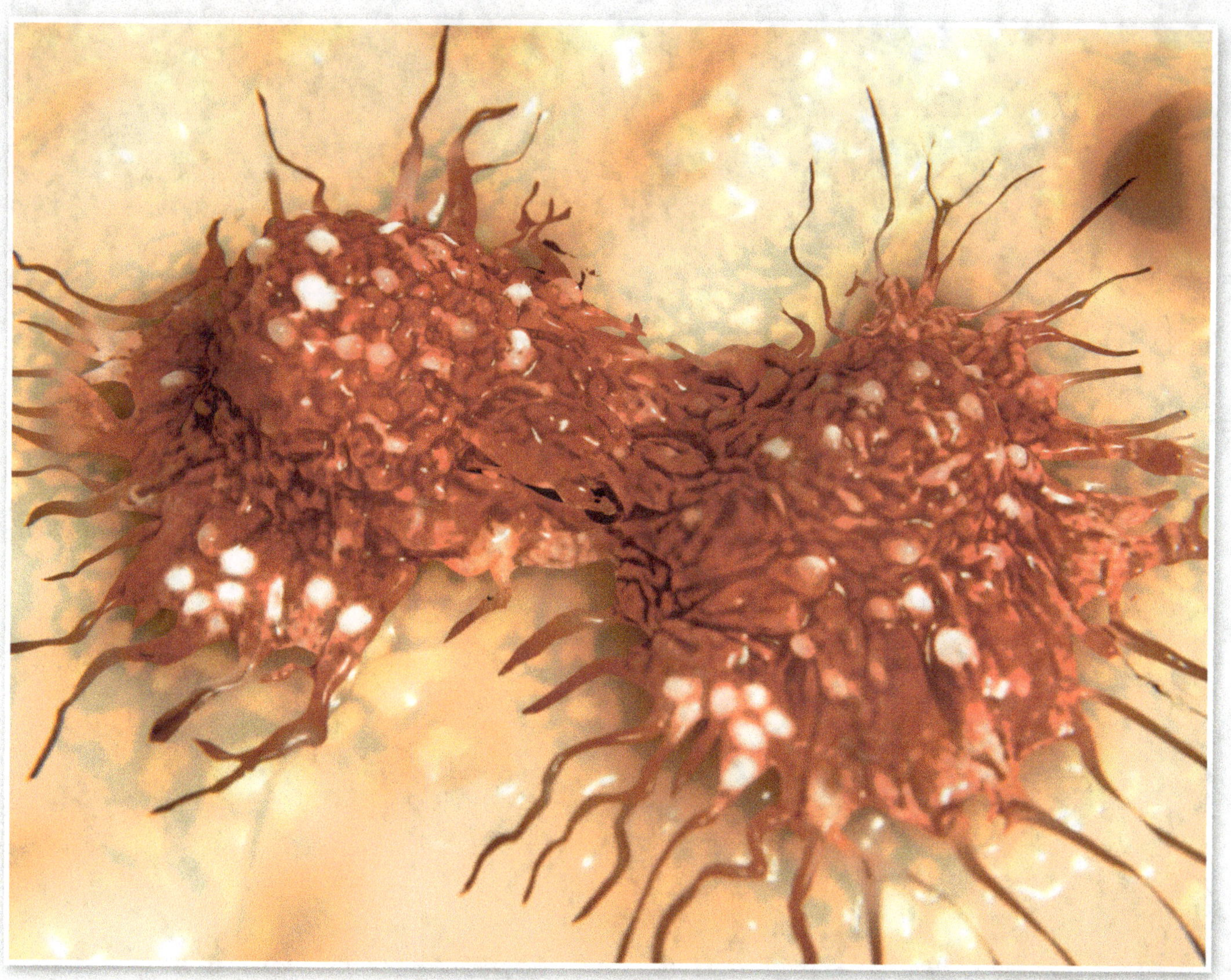

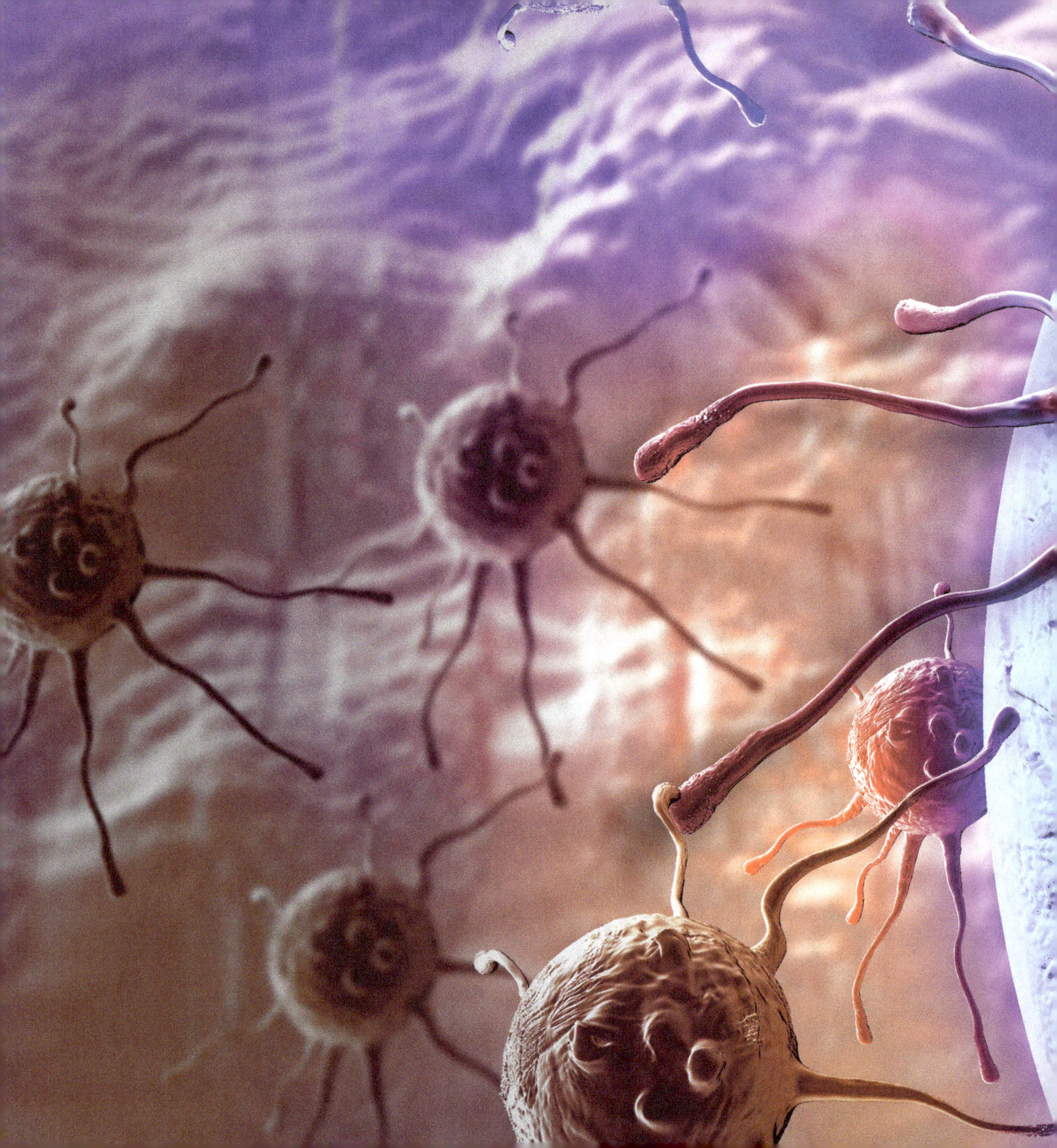

WHAT IS CANCER?
Cancer cells.

Cancer starts at the cellular level. This simply means that it begins deep within our cells. There are genes within a cell that give it instructions on how to grow and divide, but sometimes these instructions are altered or undergo mutation. This just means that they don't grow in the way they are supposed to grow normally. Most of the time the mutations have to happen more than once before an individual cell turns into cancer.

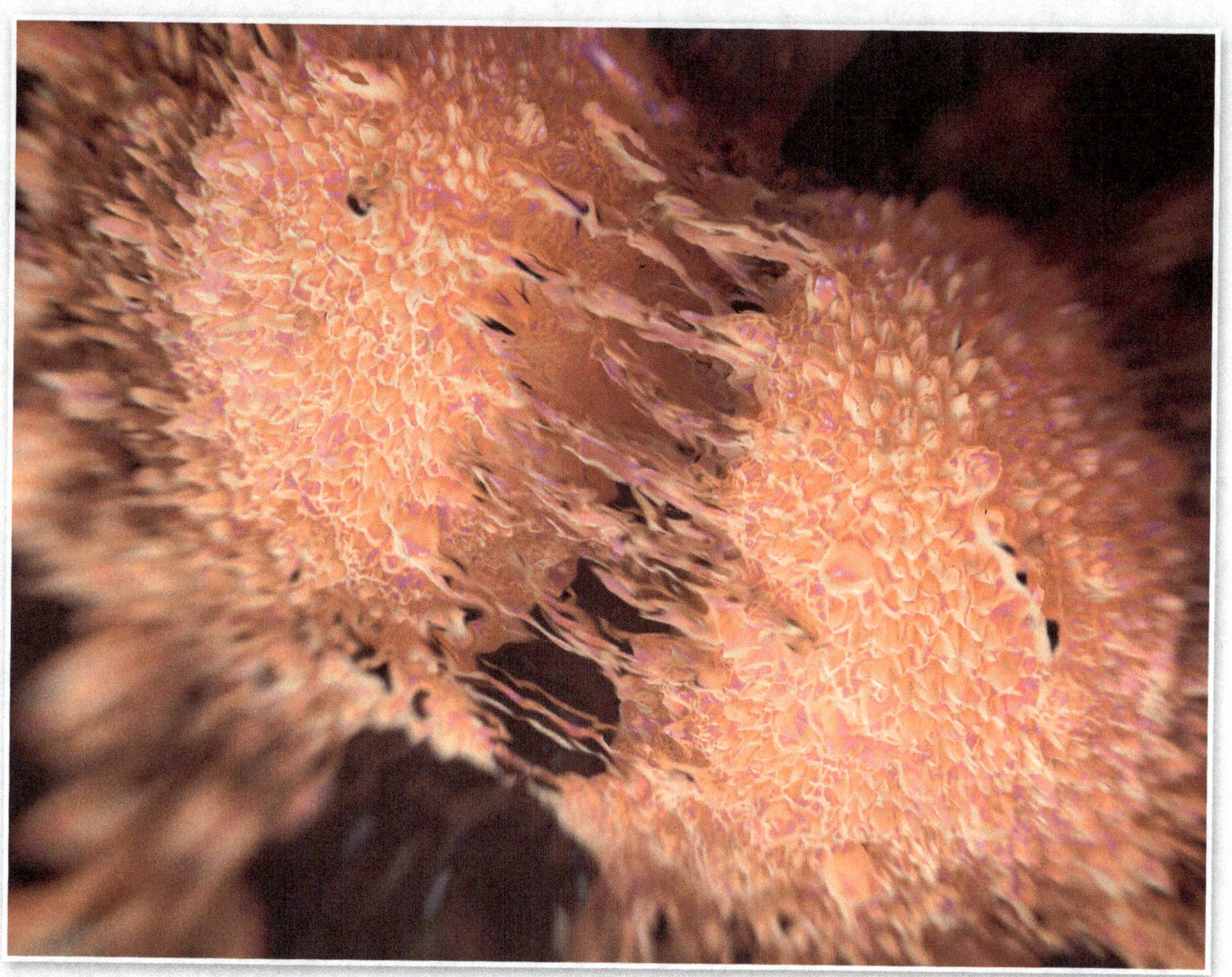

Cancer Cell Division

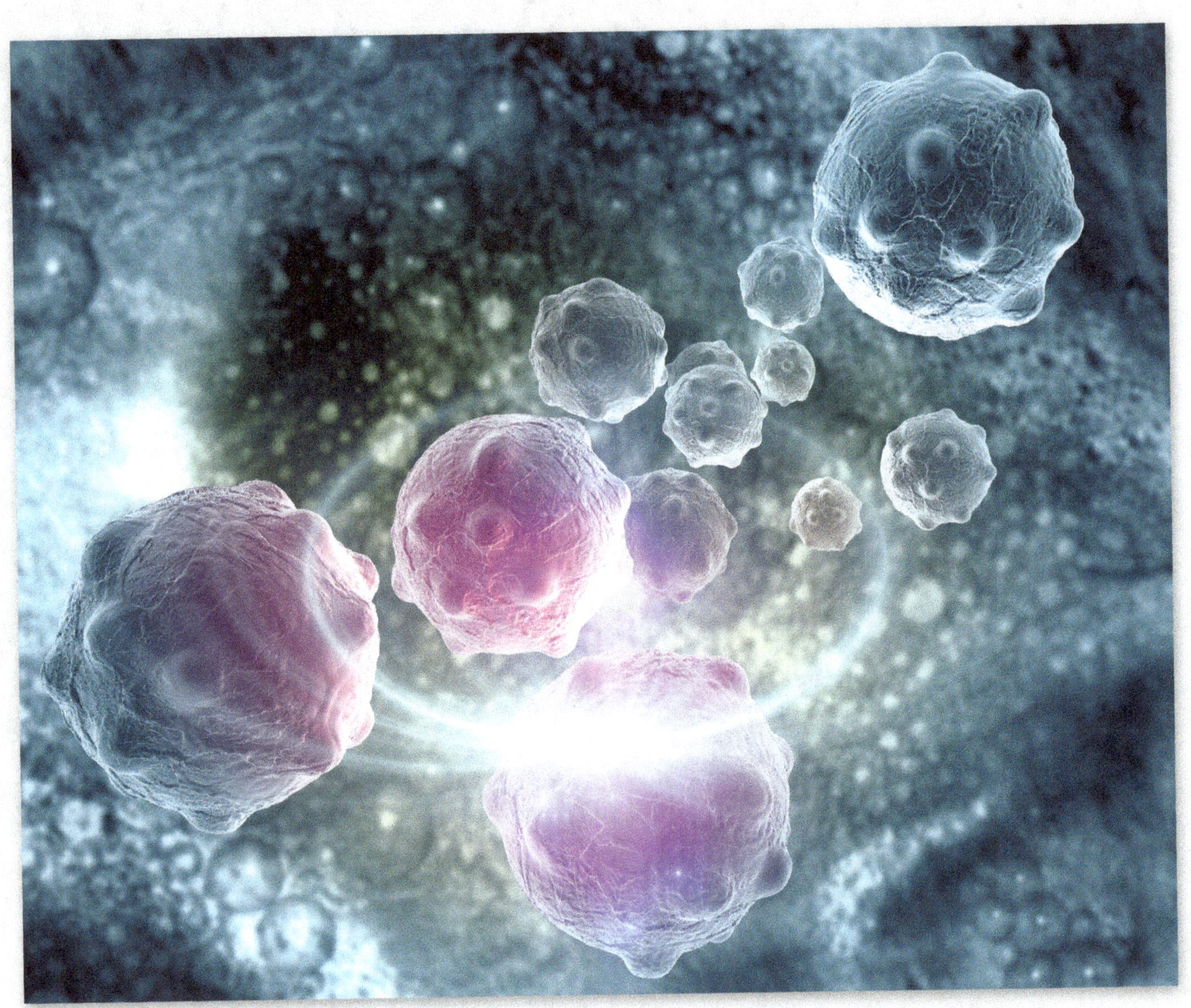

If our immune systems are strong and we're in good health, our cells will combat the mutation before the cancer can gain control. However, if the mutations continue, the cancer cells will grow in an uncontrolled way and form dangerous tumors.

Cancer Cell

WHAT CAUSES GENE MUTATIONS?

Gene mutations are caused by many different types of factors. Before you were born, you may have inherited the genes for a specific type of cancer from your parents. This type of mutation causes a small percentage of cancers. Most mutations are caused by a variety of other factors. Smoking can cause certain types of cancer.

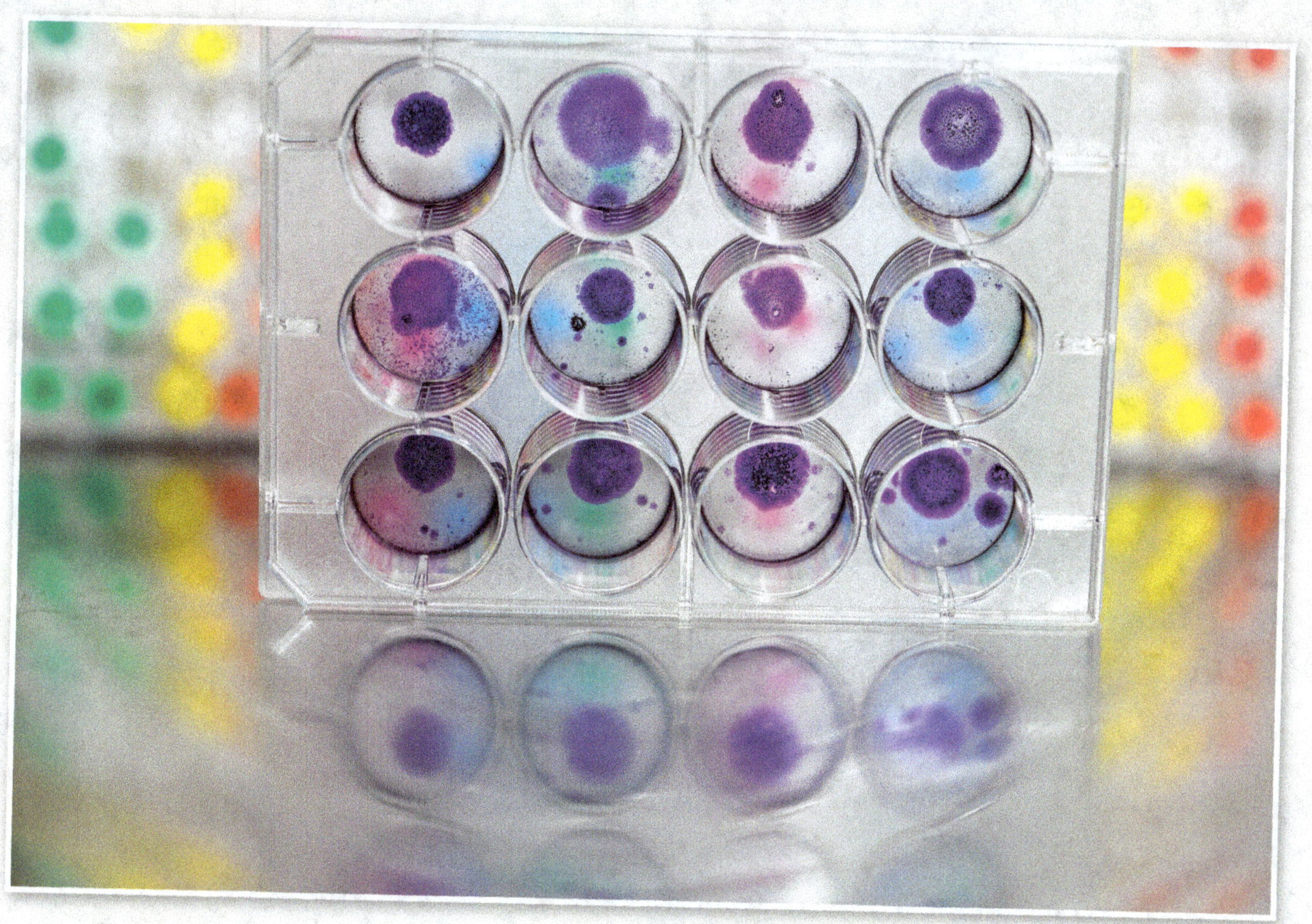

Medical Cancer Test

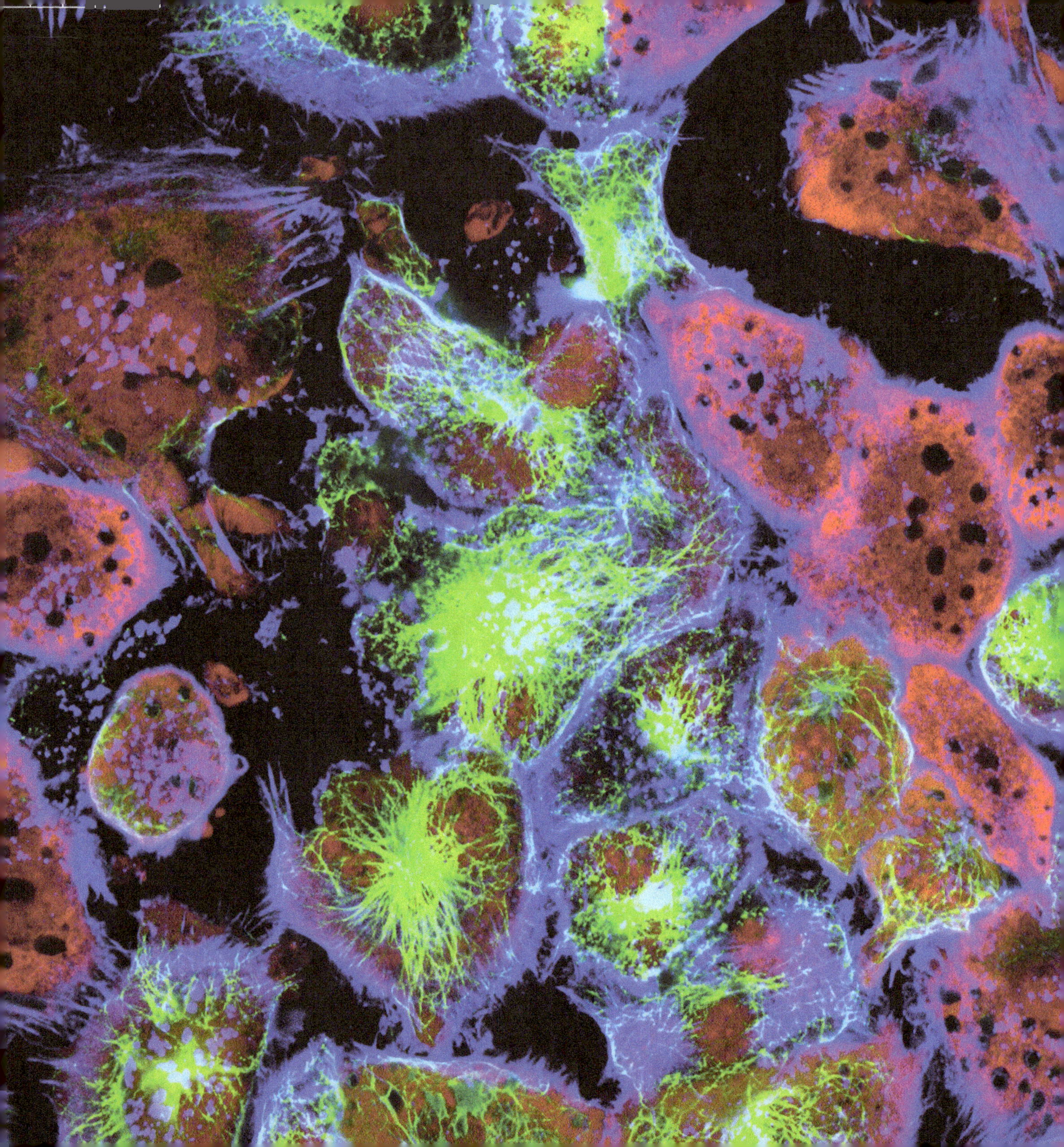

Exposure to different types of radiation or exposure to carcinogens, which are known chemicals that cause cancer, are two other ways you can get cancer. If you are obese or don't exercise, these are other risk factors for cancer. Sometimes a hormone imbalance or inflammation that happens all the time can cause cancer.

Tumor cells under microscope.

The mutations you have when you're born and those that you get during your life interact with each other to cause cancer. Sometimes people have a cancer-causing gene that they have inherited, but they don't get cancer because there are no substances in their environment that trigger it.

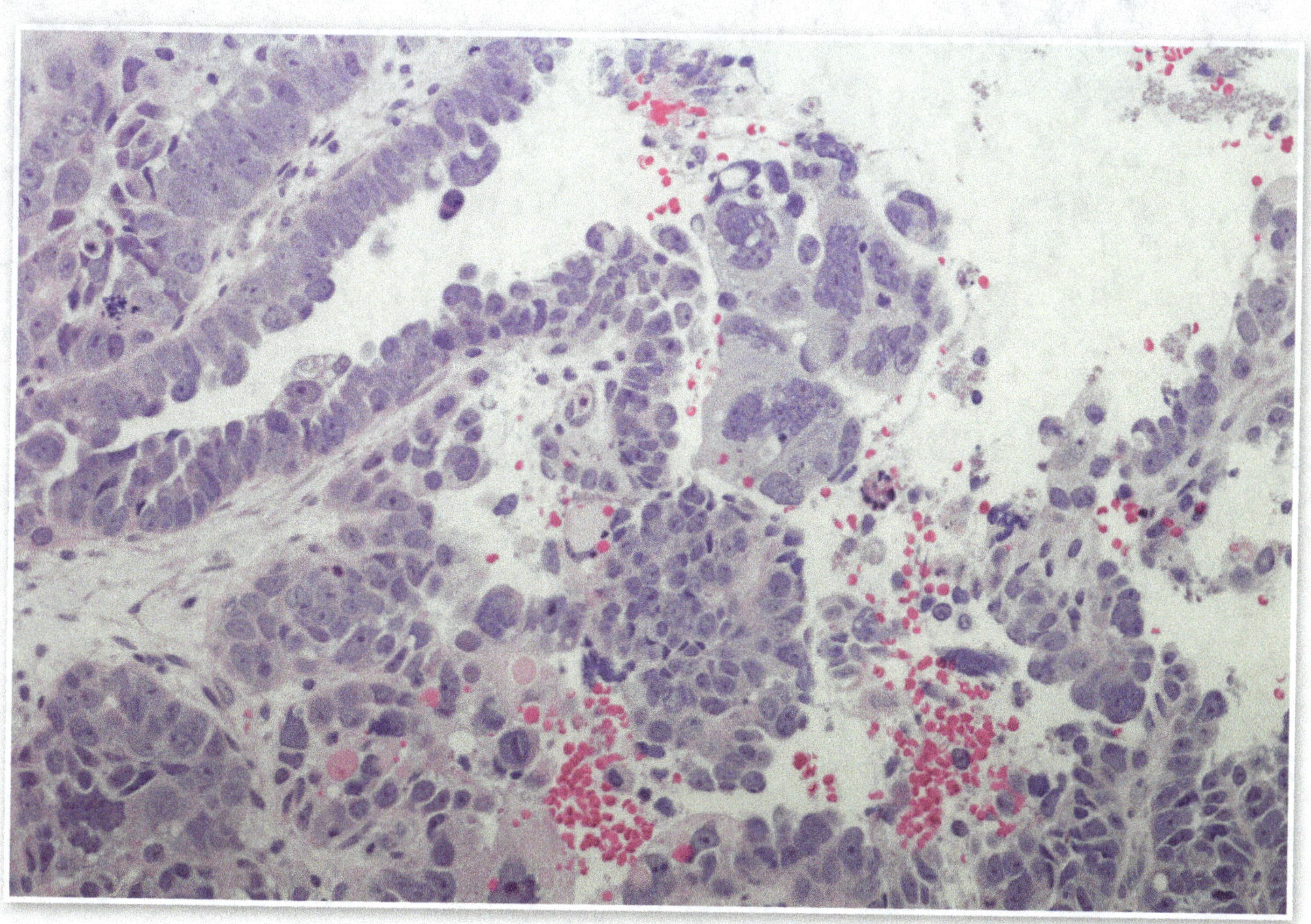

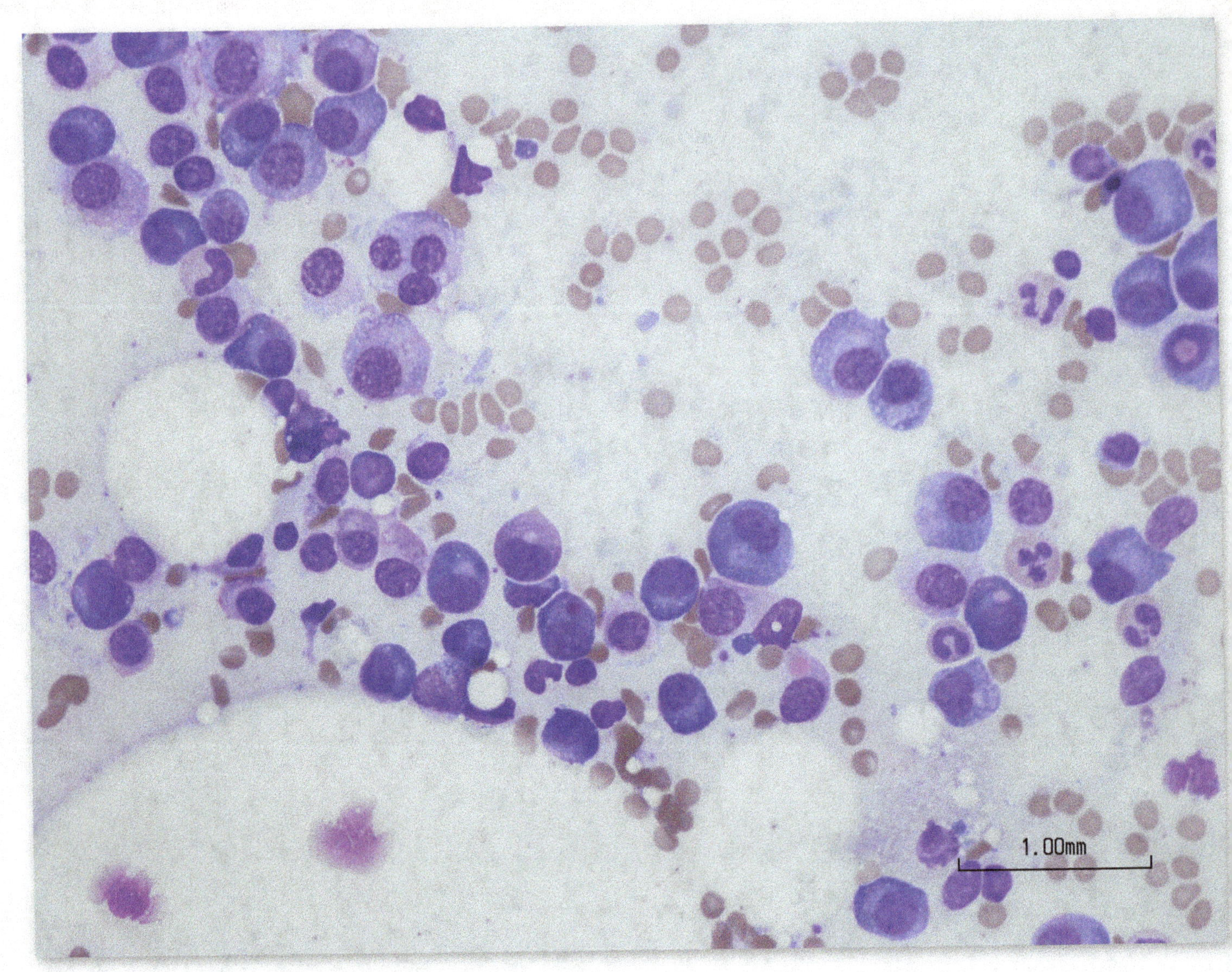

Plasma cell myeloma from bone marrow aspirate.

Cancers are typically named for the place in the body where they occur. For example, if you get a cancerous area on your skin, it's called skin cancer. Sometimes there are scientific names for the different types of cancer you can get in a particular organ. For example, there are several different types of thyroid cancer and some are more slow growing than others.

Also, sometimes cancer begins in one place in the body, but then spreads to another part, causing a secondary cancer. For example, if you have colon cancer, it can spread to your liver. The cancer you would get in your liver from the spread of colon cancer wouldn't be the same as a cancer that had originally started in your liver.

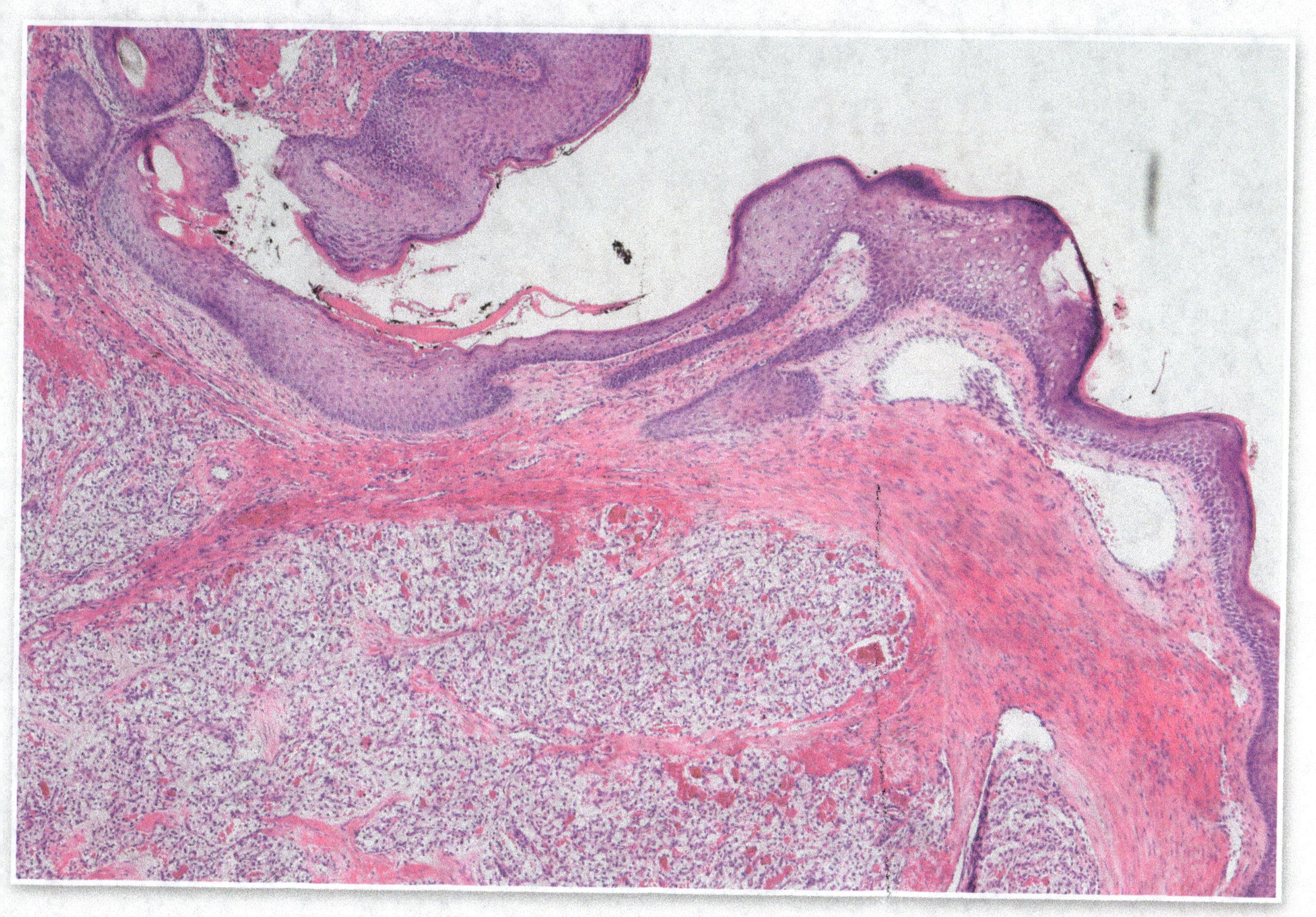

Clear Cell Renal Cell Carcinoma (CCRCC).

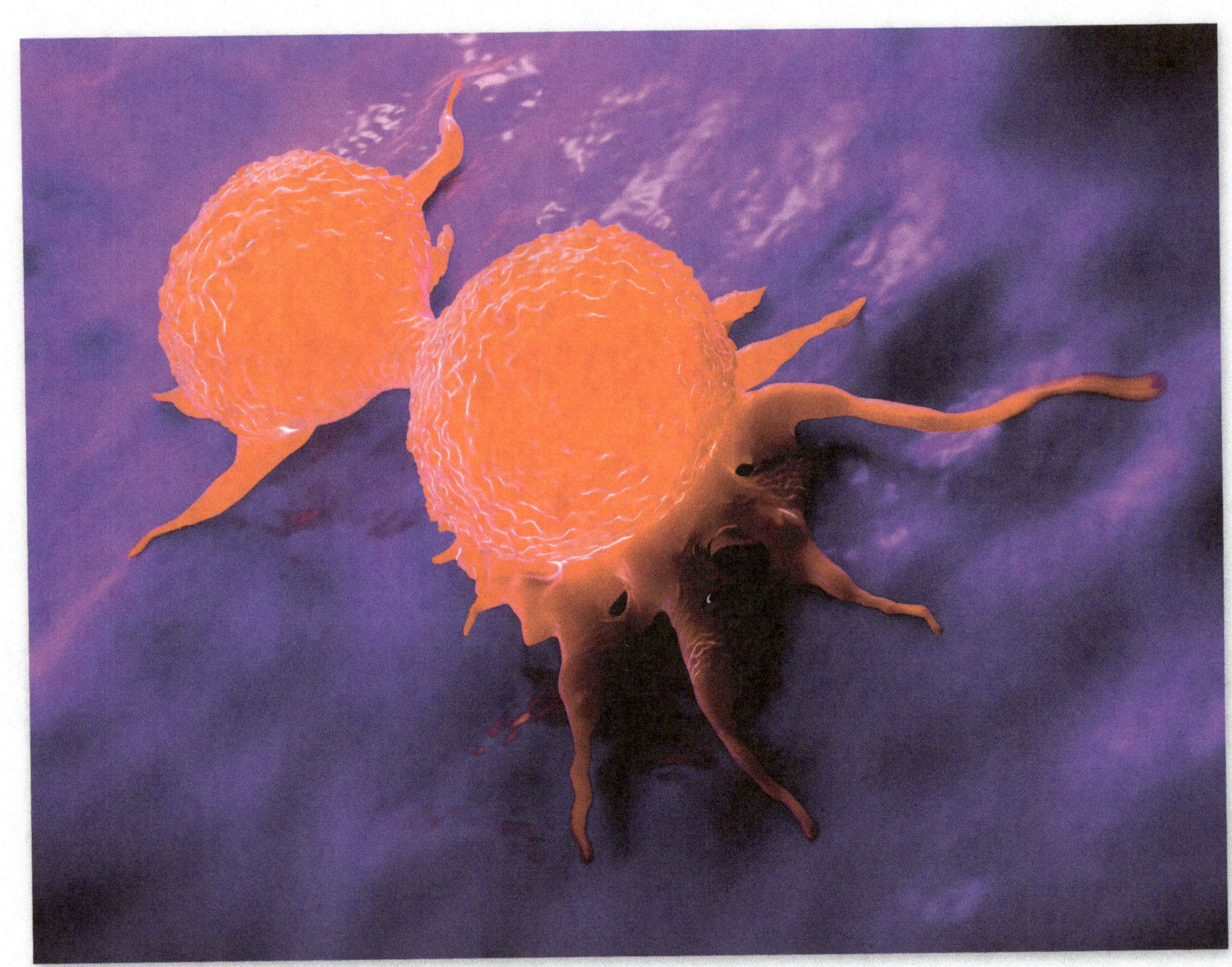

Dividing Breast Cancer Cell

BREAST CANCER

This cancer generally forms in the glands of a woman's breast. However, men can get breast cancer as well although it is rare in men. Breast cancer is very common in women and if caught early is curable. There are different forms of breast cancer and some are more aggressive than others.

COLON CANCER

This cancer forms in the colon. The colon is a section of the large intestine. Colon cancer is generally a very slow-growing cancer and a person can have it for a long period of time before any symptoms show up.

Colon Cancer Cells

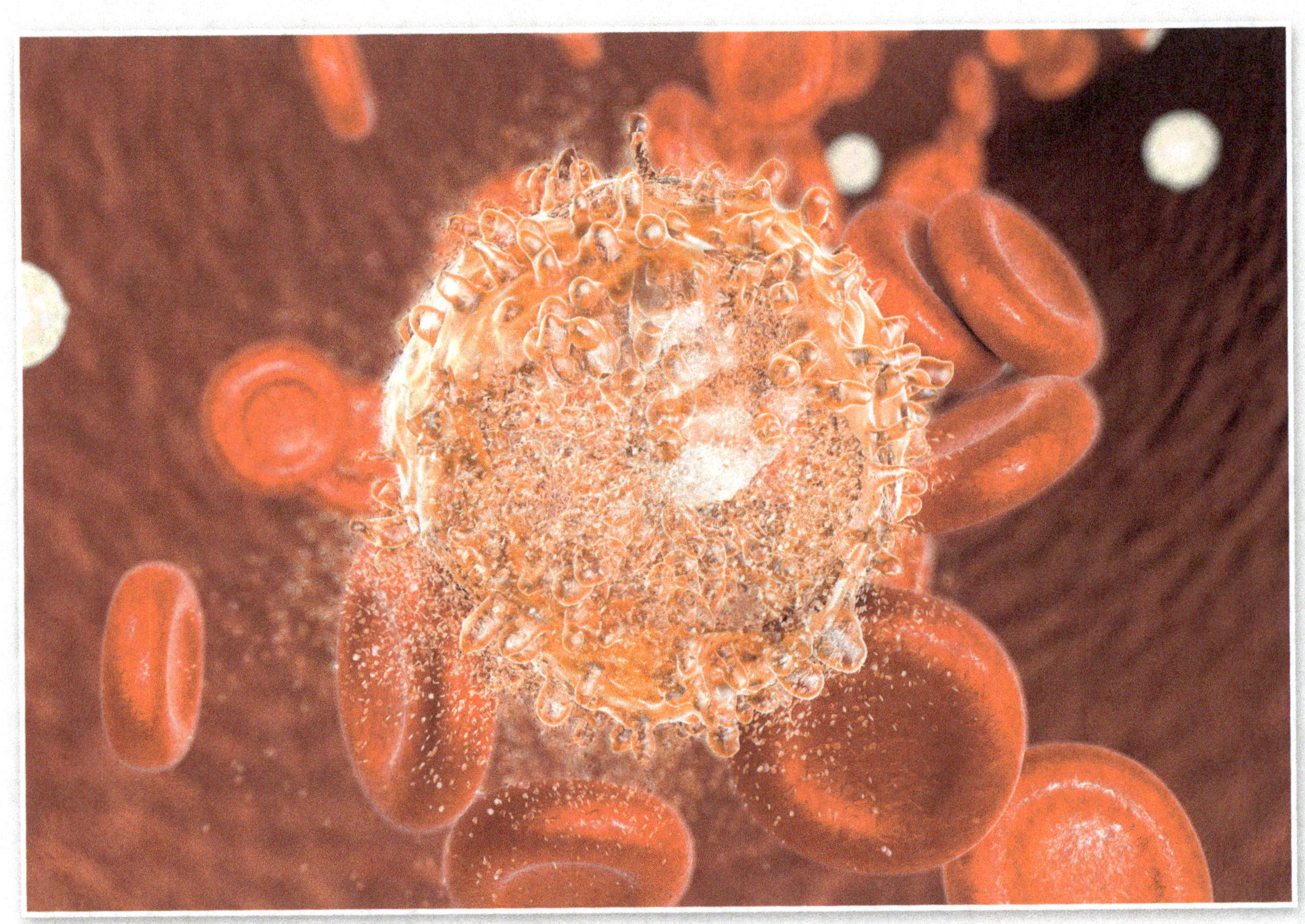

Destruction of Leukemia Cell

LEUKEMIA

Leukemia is a cancer of the organs that form blood, including bone marrow. It suppresses the normal blood cells, which leads to anemia and other symptoms. There are many different types of leukemia. Some are slow growing and others are more aggressive and grow fast.

LYMPHOMA

Lymphoma is a type of cancer that starts in the cells of the immune system that fight infection. These cells are located in different parts of the body, such as the spleen, bone marrow, and lymph nodes.

Cancer cells in lymph vessels.

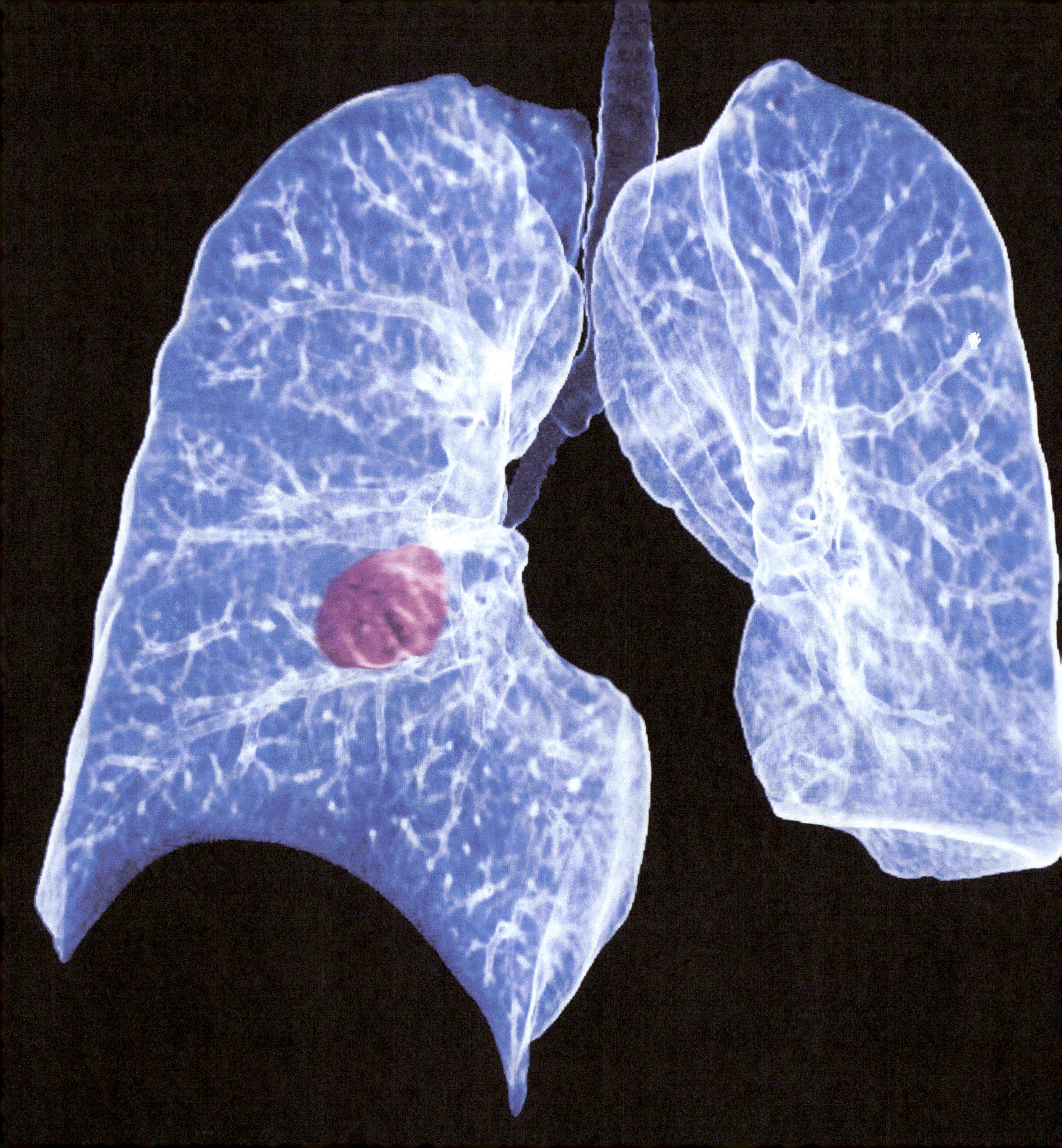

LUNG CANCER

There are several different types of lung cancer. One of the major risks of smoking is lung cancer. Exposure to secondhand smoke, diesel exhaust, asbestos, or other types of pollutants can cause lung cancer in people who don't smoke.

MELANOMA OR SKIN CANCER

Melanoma, also called skin cancer, is one of the risks of too much exposure to the rays of the sun. The pigmented portion of the eyes can also get melanoma.

PANCREATIC CANCER

Pancreatic cancer is a cancer that develops in the pancreas. This type of cancer is difficult to diagnose.

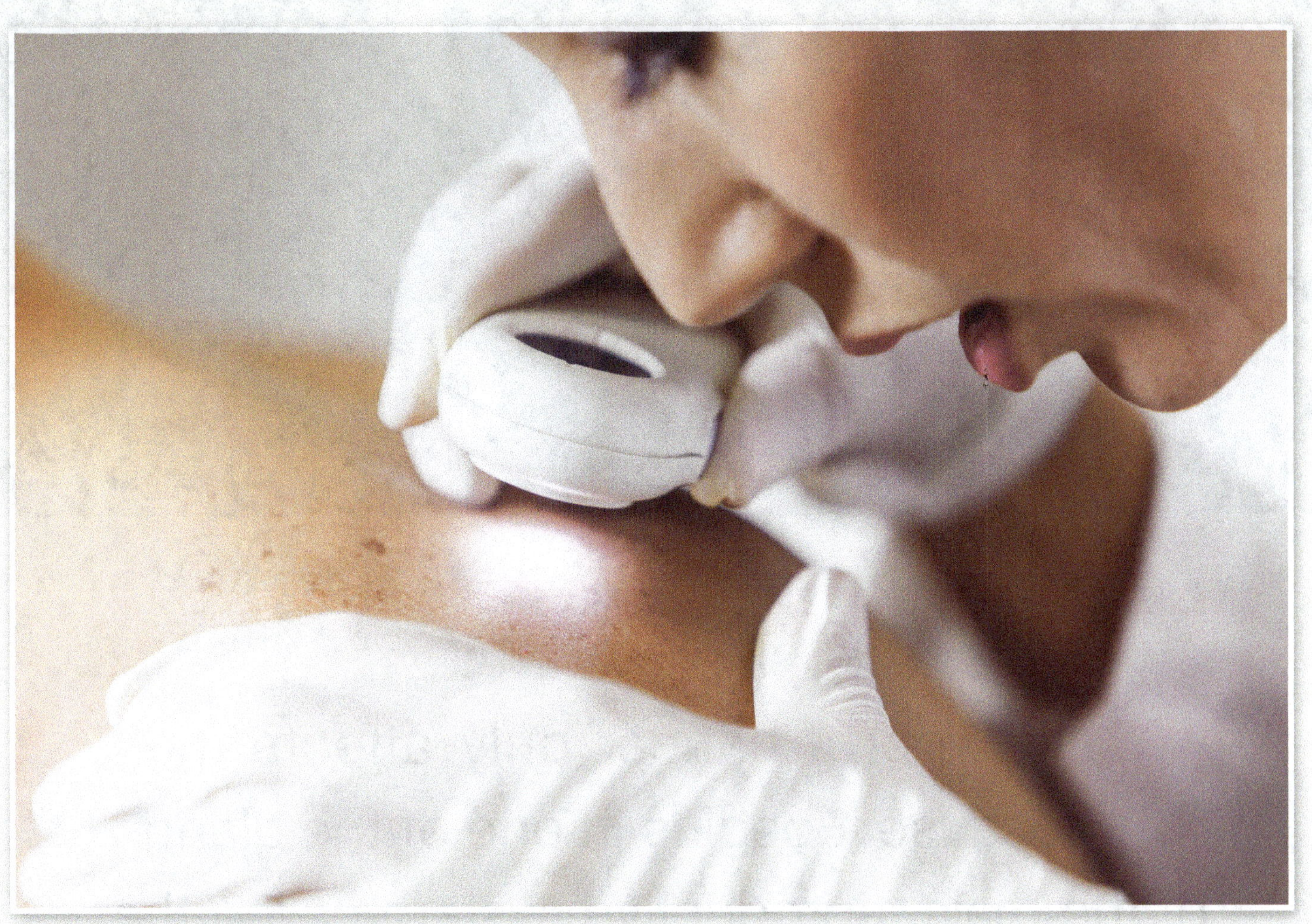

Dermatologist examining patient for
signs of skin cancer.

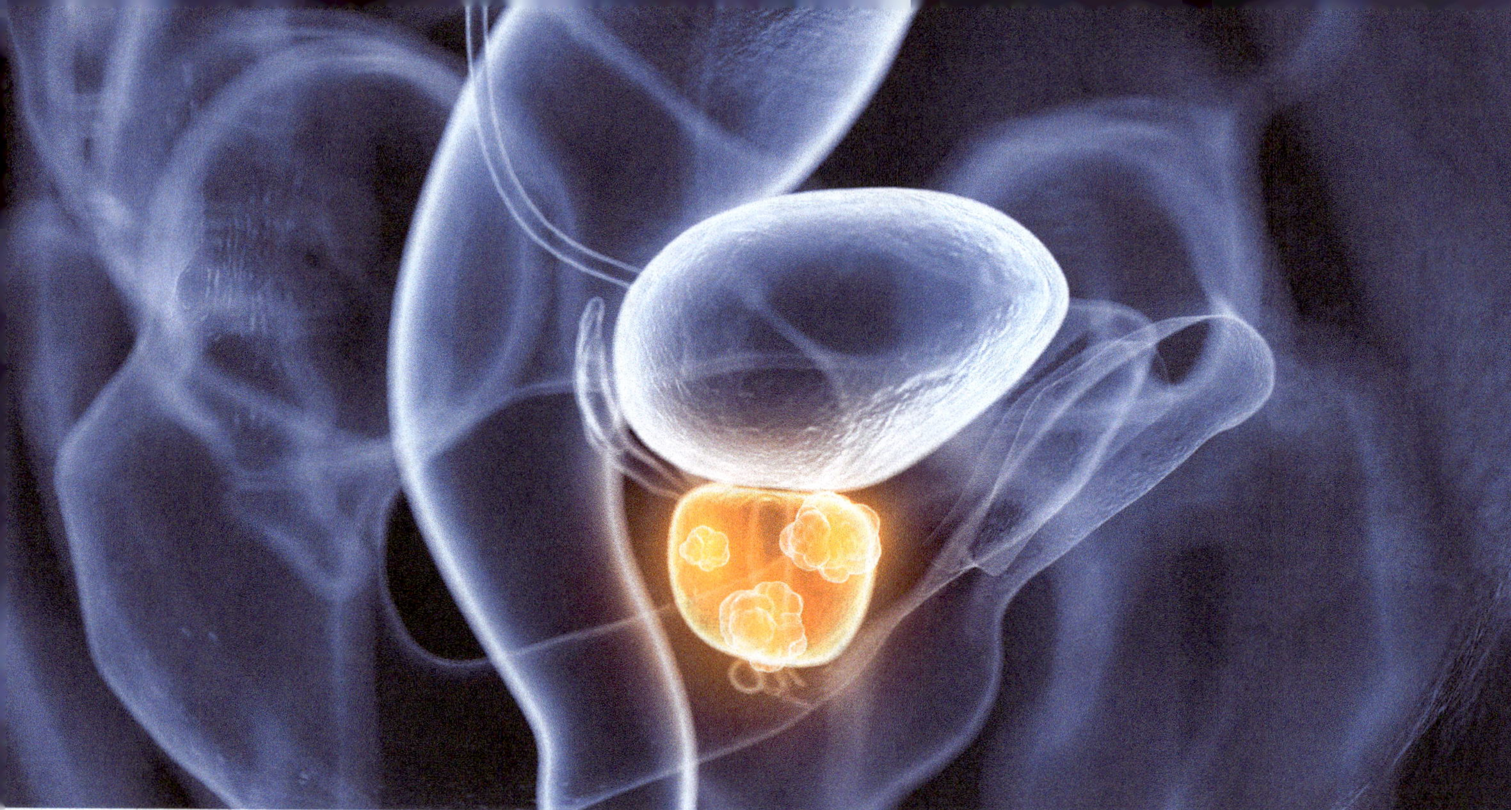

PROSTATE CANCER

This type of cancer only affects men because it begins in one of the glands of the male reproductive system called the prostate. It generally happens in older men.

Illustration of prostate cancer.

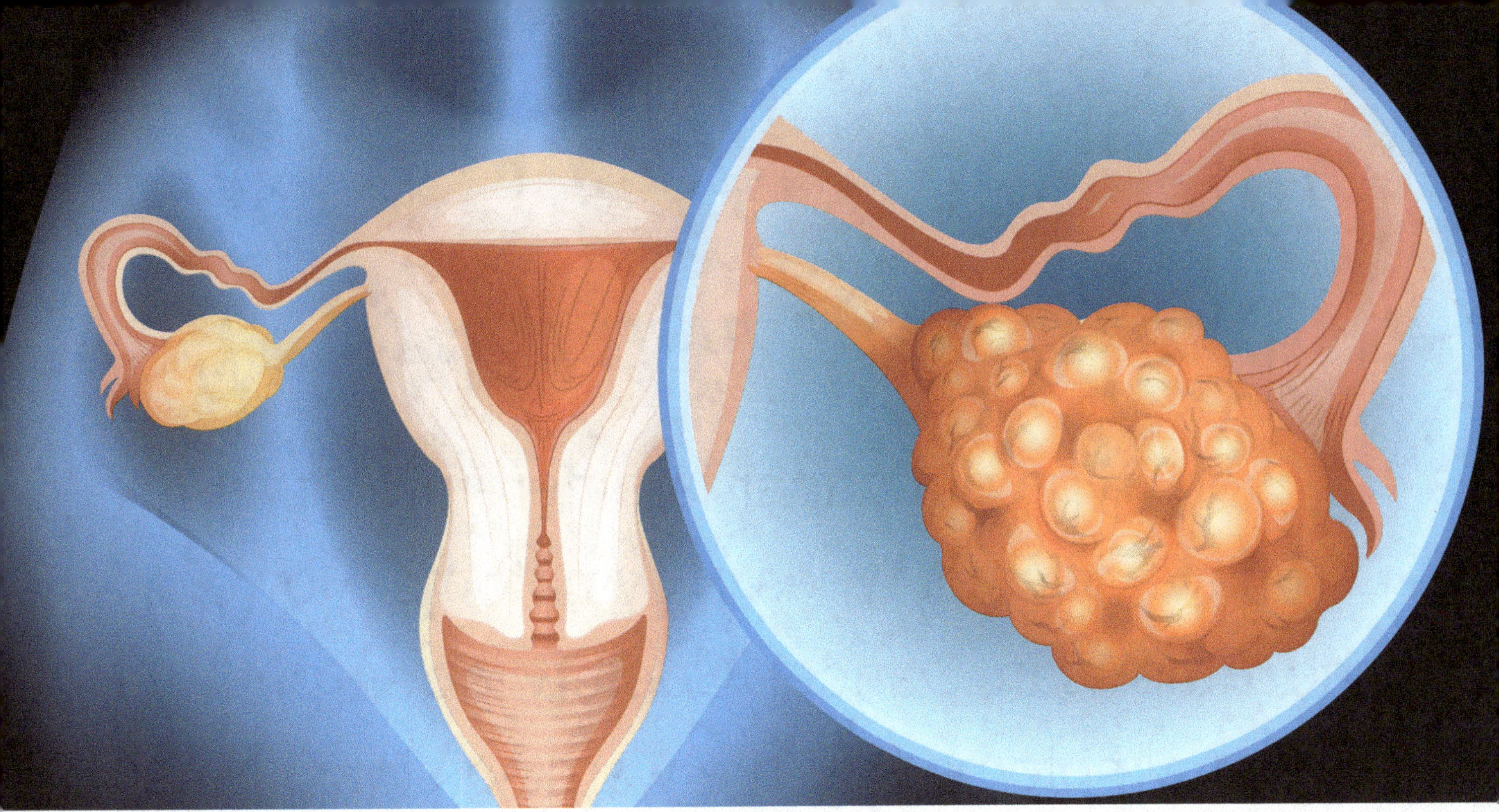

OVARIAN CANCER

This type of cancer forms only in women because it begins in the ovaries, which are the female reproductive organs that produce eggs.

Ovarian Cancer Diagram.

Every type of cancer is different so they all have different types of symptoms. However, the American Cancer Society does provide some symptoms that are warning signs. If you or someone you know is experiencing these symptoms, her or she should be checked out by a doctor.

- Any sore spot that doesn't easily heal or look normal again after a short time

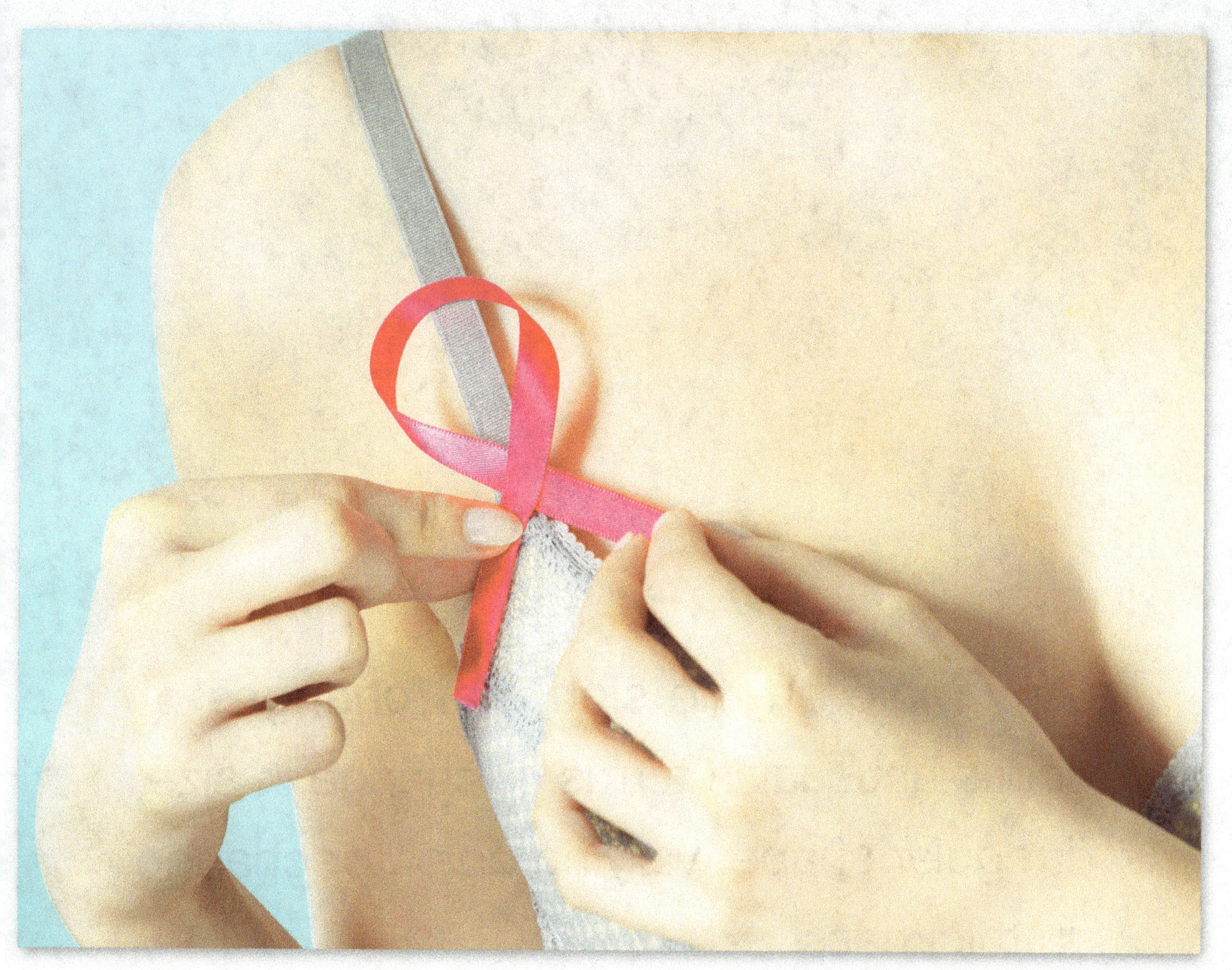

Breast Cancer Awareness Ribbon

- Any mole on the skin that changes or looks unusual in terms of change in size, irregular shape, varying color, or change in thickness

- Discomfort when swallowing or stomach upset that's chronic

- Any change in the way your bladder empties or change in your bowel movements

- Any bleeding that happens constantly or is unusual

- Any lump or growth that is thick

- A cough that happens a lot or a throat that feels scratchy

Doctors and hospitals are always working toward new treatments for cancer. There are three major types of treatments for cancer that are always being improved. In many cases, all three treatments are used to help heal the patient.

Talking with a Cancer Patient.

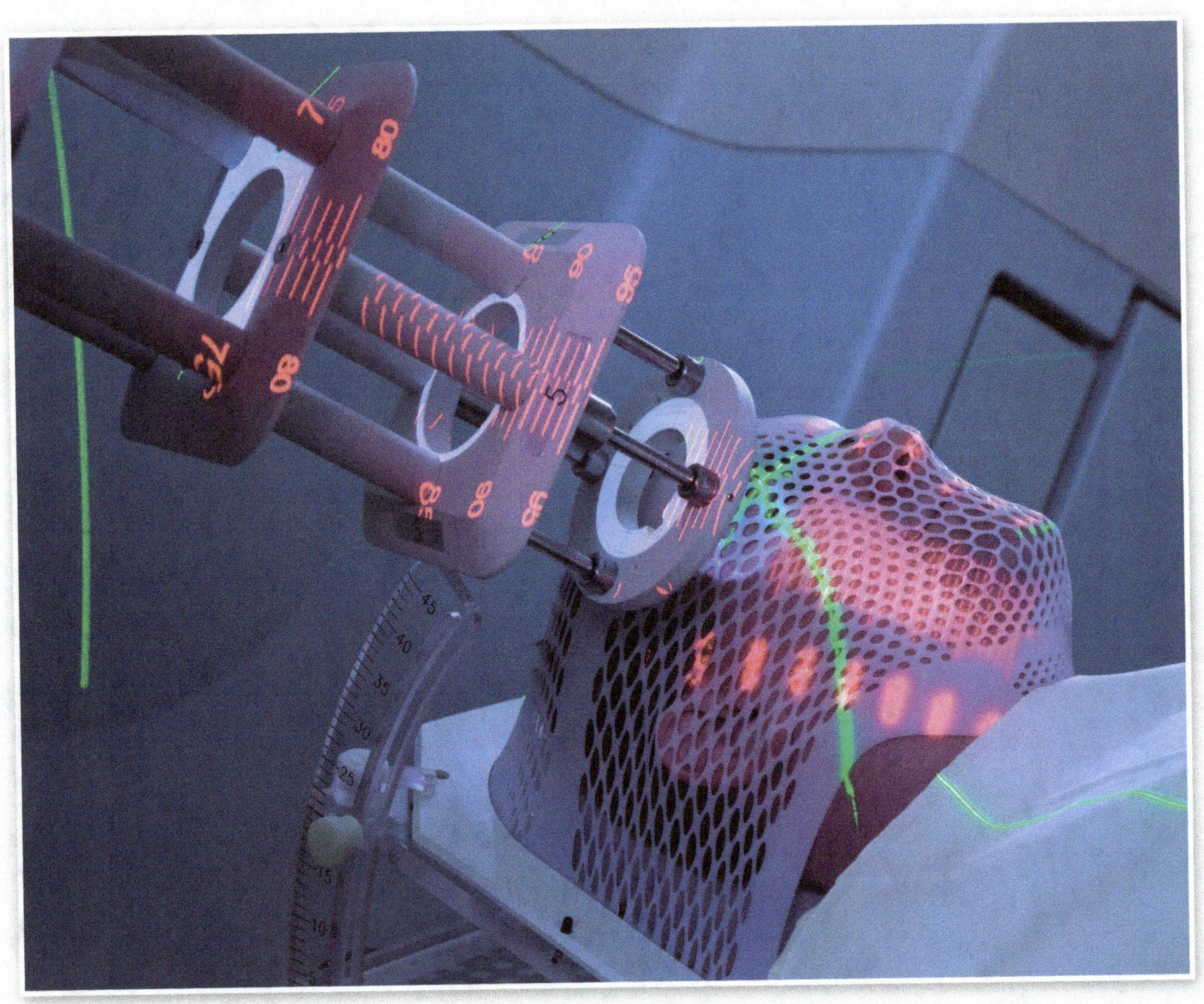

RADIATION

Radiation uses very highly focused waves of energy to pinpoint cancer cells and destroy them. It's sometimes used before surgery to reduce the size of tumors.

SURGERY

In many cases, the cancerous tumor can be located and safely removed during surgery. Lymph nodes are also frequently removed to determine whether or where the cancer has spread.

CHEMOTHERAPY

Chemotherapy uses a mixture of different chemicals to target and destroy cells that are cancerous. The chemotherapy focuses on areas of cells that are dividing rapidly as cancer cells do. The downside is that sometimes healthy tissues are destroyed as well.

Nurse preparing patient for chemotherapy.

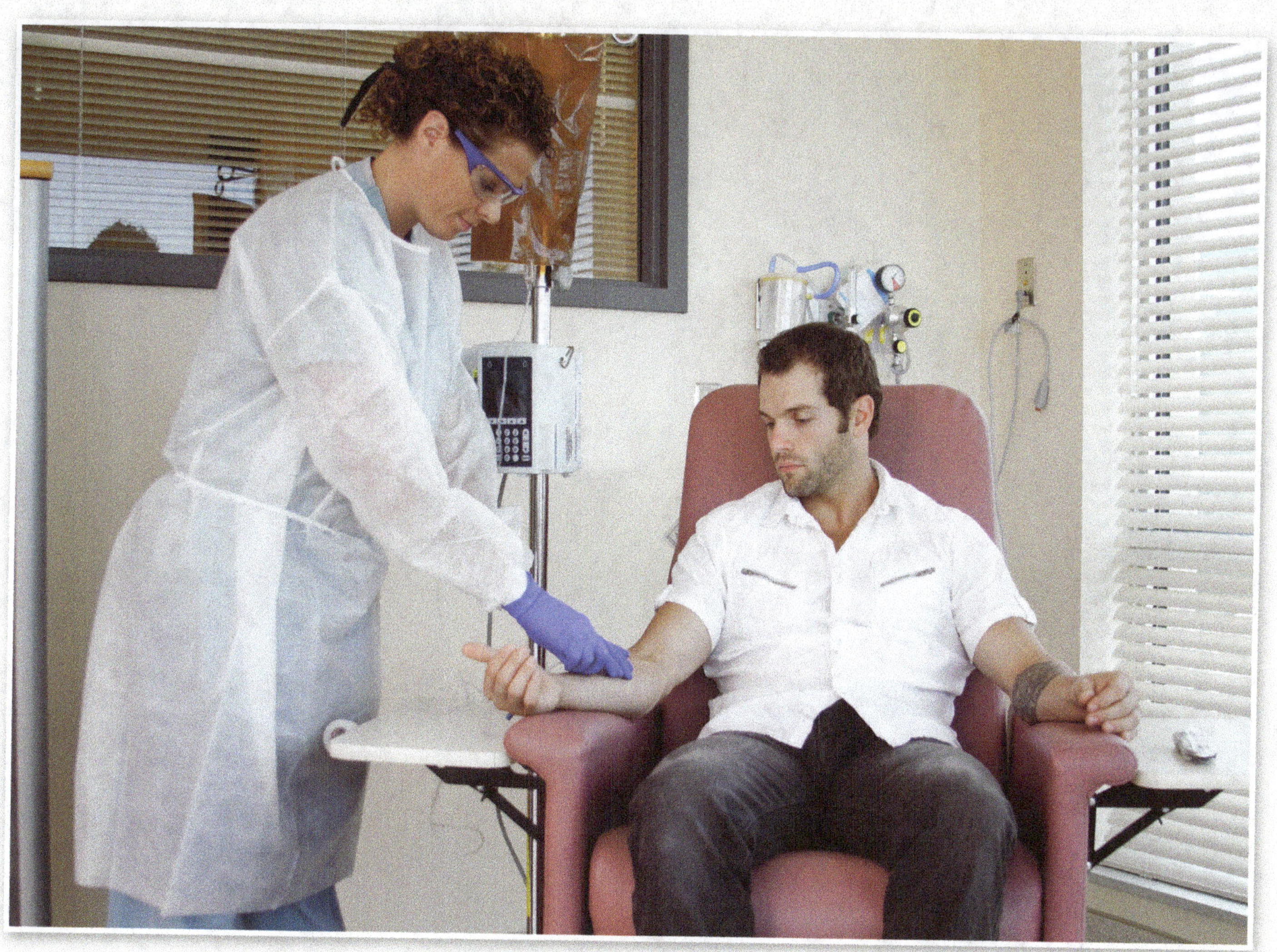

THINGS YOU CAN DO TO STAY HEALTHY AND AVOID CANCER

Here is a list of seven things you can do to help reduce your risk of getting cancer.

Breast cancer awareness pink ribbon.

MAKE A YEARLY APPOINTMENT TO SEE YOUR DOCTOR.

If something doesn't feel right, go see your doctor. A regular checkup at least once every year or if you have unusual symptoms means that your doctor might detect a problem earlier instead of later. If cancer is detected early, it can be cured.

DON'T SMOKE OR CHEW TOBACCO.

Smoking has been proven without a doubt to cause lung cancer. Chewing tobacco causes mouth cancer.

Patient laying on a CT scan platform.

EAT HEALTHY VEGETABLES AND FRUITS.

A balanced diet filled with the proper vitamins and minerals is crucial to good health. Eat plenty of dark-colored fruits and vegetables and stay away from processed foods.

Fresh fruits and vegetables.

EXERCISE REGULARLY AND MAKE SURE YOUR WEIGHT IS CORRECT FOR YOUR HEIGHT.

People who are obese are at a much higher risk for getting cancer and other diseases too. Exercise on a regular basis and maintain a healthy weight.

USE SUNSCREEN WHEN YOU GO OUT IN THE SUN.

Stay out of the sun whenever possible. If you love the beach or sitting around the pool always wear lots of sunscreen.

GET THE APPROPRIATE SHOTS FOR THE TYPES OF CANCERS WHERE IMMUNIZATIONS CAN HELP.

The human papillomavirus, called HPV for short, can cause certain types of cancers if it's inside your body a long time. You can get a vaccine that will help to prevent you from getting cervical or vaginal cancer if you're a girl. There's also a vaccine that prevents Hepatitis B, an infection that can cause liver cancer.

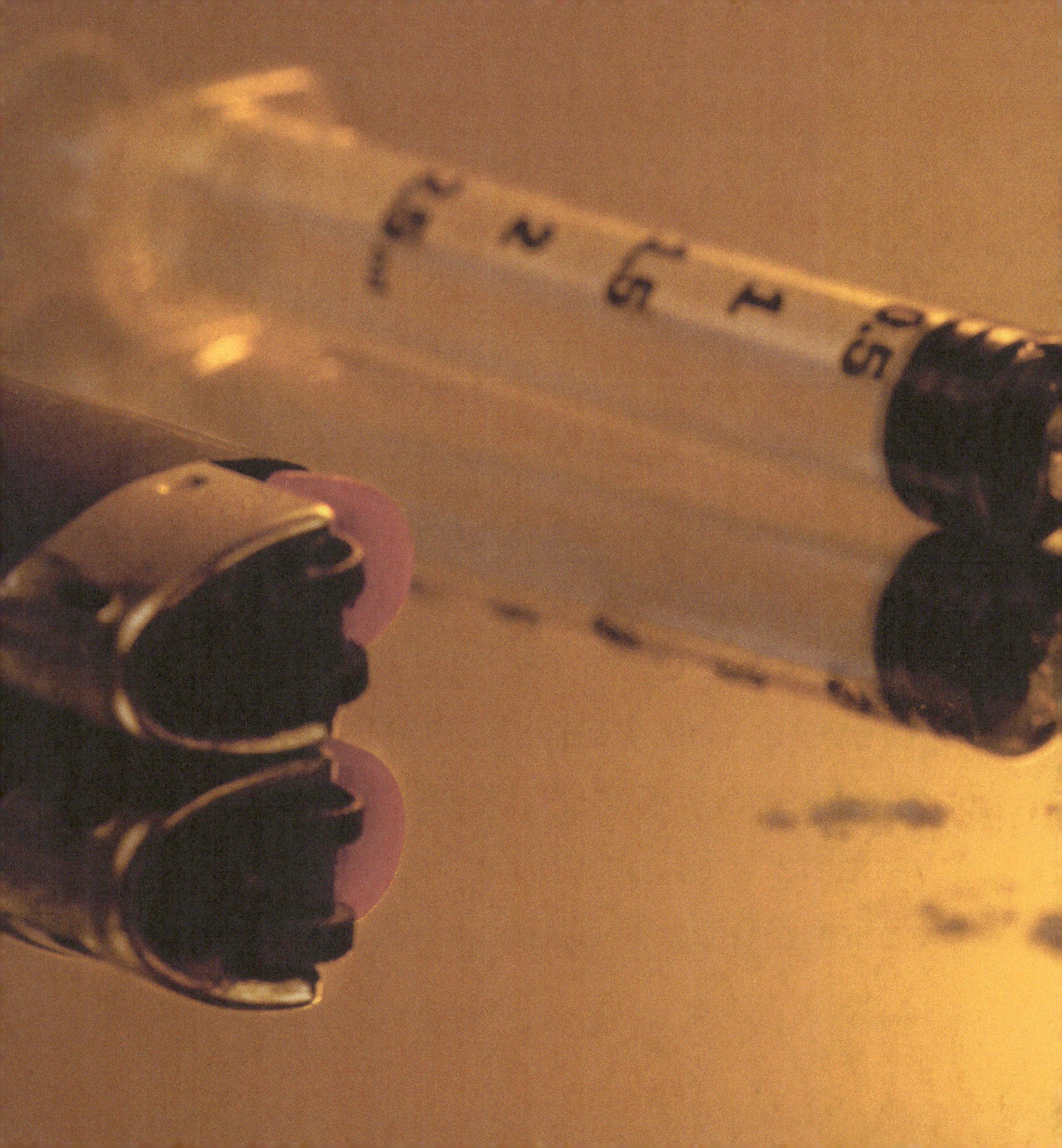

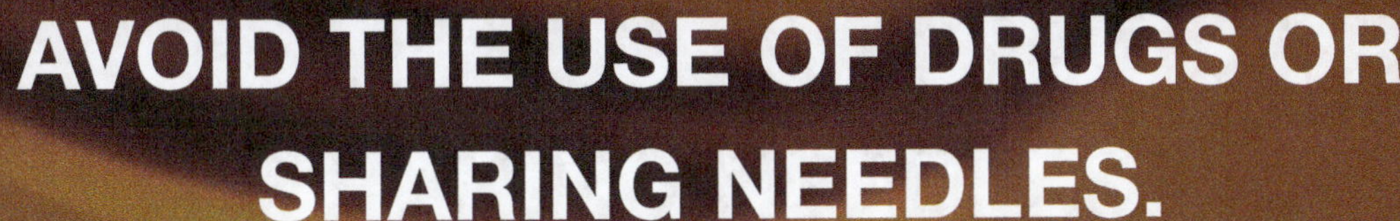

AVOID THE USE OF DRUGS OR SHARING NEEDLES.

Don't use drugs or share needles. These types of high-risk behaviors can make you vulnerable to diseases that eventually become cancer.

Now you know more about what cancer does to the body and what treatments doctors are using to help patients fight it. You can find more Biology books from Baby Professor by searching the website of your favorite book retailer.

Visit
BABY PROFESSOR
EDUCATION KIDS
www.BabyProfessorBooks.com
to download Free Baby Professor eBooks
and view our catalog of new and exciting
Children's Books